Black Woman
Coloring Book

This Book belongs to:

....

....

A. Alminiss

Love

Smiles
ARE ALWAYS
IN FASHION

—

Only
happiness

be your
OWN KIND
of
Beautiful

Powerful Woman

Only
Thank you
happiness

Focus
on the
GOOD

Never
STOP
dreaming

MAKE
Yourself
a
Priority

We hope you enjoyed our book.
As a small family company, your feedback is very important
to us.
Please let us know how you like our book at:
email: alminiss.books@gmail.com

 a.alminiss

 A.Alminiss

 a.alminiss

A.Alminiss

Made in the USA
Monee, IL
20 November 2024

70700082R00063